Curtis Curly-tail is Lizardnapped!
By Elaine A. Powers

ISBN-13: 978-1530001569
ISBN-10: 1530001560

Published by Lyric Power Publishing LLC, Tucson AZ 2015

All information provided is believed and intended to be reliable, but accuracy cannot be guaranteed by the author or the publisher.

Curtis Curly-tail is Lizardnapped!

BY

ELAINE A. POWERS

ILLUSTRATED BY
JESSICA MINNS

This book is dedicated to the plants and animals of The Bahamas
endangered by poaching,

and to the Bahamian people
who work to protect these species.

It was a dark and stormy night. Well, it had been a dark and stormy night. Now it was a bright and sunny morning. All night, lightning flashed and torrents of water flowed past my perfect den that kept me, Curtis Curly-tail, perfectly dry. Storms are common in the tropics in the summer. Storms every day, which kept the tourists away.

Without the tourists visiting me here on Warderick Wells Cay, I was bored. Every day was the same. Up with the sun, breakfast on crunchy insects, basking, watching for tourists who never came, dashing away from the gull, late afternoon insect snack, then back into my perfectly sized den to sleep.

The next summer's day was the same: hot, humid, and followed by clouds. I wandered around my territory looking for anything interesting. I had my favorite, perfectly safe spots where I watched the rain when afternoon storms popped up for a brief shower. Now and then, the gull would swoop down at me, but I always made it back to my den in time.

Almost always.

A few days ago, the gull approached me from behind, but I ran confidently toward my den. I didn't worry because I knew I'd make that last dash for safety as the gull dove down at me.

I made the perfect final lunge but the entrance to the den was blocked! Rainwater had swirled the sand down around the entrance. Instead of my flat opening, there was a sand dune!

I dug frantically as I heard the ruffle of feathers. Dirt flew from my perfect, rapidly digging hands. I flung myself into my den just as I heard the snap of the gull's beak and the swoosh of the wings.

I was afraid to look at my curled tail, convinced the gull had snipped off the end curl. Finally, I looked… and my tail was…perfect. My tail wasn't eaten. I know my tail detaches to help me escape predators and that it will grow back, but it was perfect the way it was. I didn't want a regenerated tail. For several days, I stayed close to my den, only going a little way out to bask in the sun and back in when the rain fell.

Now, I was bored again. No tourists to greet. No hutia to ride. No boats to watch. I longed for an adventure. I'd even be willing to take a short trip on one of the boats that brought the humans, either tourists or scientists. Only it'd have to be a short trip. One where I could leave first thing in the morning, after breakfast ,of course, and return to my own den at sundown.

Then it happened. I was looking under dried leaves searching for anything interesting when I heard it. The sound of a boat engine. The tourists were coming!

I ran down to the beach to welcome them. I was so excited, I forgot for a minute that a perfect curly-tail lizard waits for the humans to come to him. I retreated up the sand dune a little ways until I found the perfect rock to climb on and pose. I wanted to welcome these visitors with my best possible, my perfect, pose.

These didn't look like the humans who usually visit my cay. Usually, they wear swim suits. A few times, scientists came wearing work clothes and hiking boots. These people getting out of their inflated boat on the beach were dressed half-way between the two. Some wore jeans and t-shirts, some wore shorts, but they were all men. All the boats before had had some women. Well, I don't discriminate. All were welcome to admire me.

They stood on the beach, passing out cloth bags. No cameras or towels or clipboards. Like the scientists who came to study the hutia, these men carried poles and nets. I wondered if they were here to check on the hutia. Maybe they came to study other animals. Maybe they were here to study us curly-tails. Wouldn't that be exciting?

"We'll go over to the beach on the other side," said the man with a beard. I've always been interested in beards. How do the humans get the scales on their faces to grow that way? I moved closer to get a better look. I was perfectly quiet so they wouldn't notice me. I sensed these humans weren't here to photograph me.

"How many d' we want?" a thin man asked. He was so thin, he reminded me of that poor curly-tail Clive who lives under the dead bushes on the far side of the cay.

"As many as we can catch," Bearded-Man replied. "You got bait?

"Yeah," a man with long-hair replied. His long hair reminded me of the tail feathers of a White-tailed Tropic bird.

"Meet back here at high tide."

"I've got a net and a noose; we're set," Long-Hair said. Bearded-Man and Thin-Man headed down the beach and over the sand dunes. The remaining two men stood looking at the dunes in my direction. The fourth man had a smooth shiny head. It reminded me of the moon-shells I've seen on the beach. I didn't think they could see me, camouflaged against the limestone karst rocks and sand. Then my eyes met the eyes of Long-Hair. He nudged the bald man with his elbow and lifted his chin in my direction.

"Let's get to it," he said. Bald-Man, took a bag out of his pocket. He reached into it and pulled something out, tossing it in my direction.

I didn't recognize what he'd thrown toward me. I was curious. I took a few steps closer. An interesting odor wafted in the breeze. How intriguing. I took a few more steps closer. It smelled edible. Yes, definitely edible.

I like trying new foods. I took a few more steps. I peered at the piece of food. I looked at it with both of my perfect eyes, then cocked my head to each side to check it out with one eye at a time. I dashed forward, intending to quickly grab the item and retreat to a safe distance.

But as my mouth closed around the very tasty morsel, something pulled tight around my neck. In my fascination with the food, I hadn't noticed Bearded-Man kneeling down holding a stick with a piece of rope at the end.

"Good job, man," said Long-Hair. "You're really good with that noose." He grabbed me with his hand and shoved me head first into a cloth bag. He tied the top of the bag shut. I, Curtis Curly-tail, the perfect curly-tail lizard of Warderick Wells, was being lizardnapped!

With me trapped inside, Long-Hair started walking. I wondered if he was looking for more lizards. For what seemed to be hours and hours, I bounced along as he walked. I explored the entire length and breadth of the bag hoping to find a way out. A small hole would have been perfect. I can squeeze through most small holes. I ran up the side of the cloth and tried to push out the top. Sadly, I couldn't find any way out, so I bounced and bounced and bounced.

Every now and then, the man would stop and move very slowly. I imagined him creeping up on another of my fellow Warderick Wellians. Were the men capturing only curly-tails or were other animals in danger? I hadn't seen any cages like the scientists had used with the hutia, but that didn't mean they didn't have them. I told myself to have patience. I expected to find out what was going on…eventually.

The day got hotter and hotter. I longed for the shade of my den so I could thermoregulate and keep my body at the pleasant perfect temperature. The air got more humid. I was very uncomfortable. I was about to make one more run up the inside of the bag to the top when I heard the crack of a lightning bolt nearby and the loud, ominous rumble of thunder. Surely, Long-Hair would find shelter. Any sensible curly-tail, especially a perfect one like me, knows to take shelter in a storm.

Soon the rain drops began to fall. The air temperature dropped to a nice level, so I was glad of that. The bag was getting get wetter and wetter. Obviously this human didn't have the sense of a curly-tail.

Soon the bag was soaked! I didn't mind the wetness, but air couldn't pass through the soaked cloth of the bag. I, Curtis Curly-tail, was going to suffocate!

Then the man must have started running, because I was being bounced against his body quite roughly. If I was going to suffocate, at least let me go in peace, quietly, listening to the sounds of my cay. The tie at the top of the bag loosened a bit and fresh air, well, rain-soaked air, flowed in. I wasn't going to suffocate, but I might be bounced to death. I did not like this human at all. I wrapped my tail around my body and kept my limbs tucked in tight.

We must have reached the beach because Long-Hair slowed down and I could hear the waves crashing violently. I shared the waves' anger. What was happening to me was not right!

"Let's get back to the boat," I heard one of the men say. I heard the waves slapping against the inflated boat as my captor climbed in, and I felt the bouncing as we went over waves. Once again I was leaving my perfect cay of Warderick Wells! Before, I had always returned, but I had a bad feeling about this trip. This trip might just be one way, taking me away from my home forever.

After a short time, the bag was lifted up and tossed onto a hard surface.

"Careful, man. Don't injure them or we won't get our money," said one of the men. "We can't sell broken lizards."

The bag I was in was lifted again and turned upside down, and I was shaken out of the bag into a cage. The spaces in the mesh were very small. There was no way even a perfect curly-tail like myself could fit through those holes.

After trying to pry open the side of the cage, I looked around and saw that I was not alone. There were other curly-tail lizards in the cage with me.

"Hello, Curtis," came a voice from the corner. "It's me, Clive."

Clive? Clive, the thin curly-tail from the area of Warderick Wells where the plants that had been damaged by the hutia? Clive, the not-so-perfect curly-tail, but still wonderful curly-tail?

"Clive! It's so good to see you. I never expected to see you again. You were so thin and hungry."

"I stayed under the dead bushes in my little territory. I found enough food to stay alive. You're more knowledgeable than me, Curtis. What's happening to us?"

"I don't know. I was watching the men on my beach and then they caught me and stuck me in a bag."

"They put out some orange peels for me. I was hungry. Ha, I'm always hungry and the orange smelled so good. It tasted good, too. Suddenly, a net came down over me. I felt a hand close around my body. I thought I was going to be crushed. But you want to know something, Curtis?"

"Yes," I replied.

"That orange peel was so good, I didn't really mind being captured. Maybe they'll feed us some more orange. Until they do, I'll hang on to this piece of peel. You know what else?"

"No, what?"

"I wouldn't mind living any place where they have such wonderful food."

"But Clive, even though the food might be good, you'll be trapped. You'll never run free again. Curly-tails need to run free."

"Maybe you do, Curtis, you're a perfect curly-tail. Me? I could do well in captivity, I think."

"No, don't think that way, Clive. We've got to escape."

"All right, but let's wait until after they feed us."

That sounded like a reasonable idea, so I agreed with Clive. He searched the cage for food, while I studied the boat and the humans. I needed to know as much as I could for my great, no, my perfect, escape.

Wham! The loud noise startled me and the rest of the curly-tails.

"Let me out of here," a loud voice said. Where was it coming from?

Wham! "Let me out now!" The voice sounded female…and large.

Wham! I realized the sound was coming from inside a storage box on the deck beside our cage.

Wham!

Bearded-Man said, "Hey, go find out what's going on with that iguana. Make sure they can't get out." Thin-Man walked over to the box. He checked the lid and the sides. Then he gave the box a hard kick.

"You shut up in there." The other men laughed. I looked at Clive. I felt the fear I saw on Clive's face.

"We made a pretty good haul this trip, mates," Bald-Man said.

"That we did," Bearded-Man agreed.

"We taking them to one place or making several stops?" Thin-Man asked.

"You ask a lot of questions, you know that?" Bearded-Man said.

"Hey, I want to know what the plans are. You know, in case you fall overboard in one of the storms."

"Well, you better make sure I don't."

A full moon shone down on the men as they relaxed on the boat deck. Suddenly, dark clouds surged across the sky. The wind blasted saltwater across the men and the boat. It was going to be another dark and stormy night. Bearded-Man used some rope to tie the curly-tail cage to the table, which was bolted to the cabin. The men gathered their items and took refuge in the cabin, and the wind called after them with a low moaning sound. Maybe this was the sound of the lost souls. Maybe this was the island mourning her lost children, her kidnapped curly-tails.

The wind blew fiercely across the deck. Waves smashed into the hull and washed over the deck.

"Curtis?"

"Yes, Clive?" I replied.

"Are we going to be washed overboard?"

"Of course not. At least I hope not."

The lizards worried all night. Some of them huddled together and entwined their curling tails. In case they ended up in the water, maybe they could hold on to each other and make a raft of themselves.

I tried not to think about being in the water with all those hungry fish. I hoped that if I did fall in, it would at least be a perfect fish who ate me. A predator worthy of eating the perfect curly-tail. I noticed that Clive hadn't eaten his piece of orange peel, but was still holding on to it. Maybe he could use it to stay afloat if we did get washed overboard.

8

For hours and hours, the storm raged. Waves continued to wash over the deck. The men huddled inside the cabin. I realized it was kind of like my den. Oh, how I missed my perfect den that night. Instead of my body fitting perfectly into a safe place, I was out in the open being sprayed by salt water. I don't mind admitting I was scared. Cold and scared. What had the world come to when Curtis Curly-tail was cold and scared?

The sun, the wonderful perfect sun, arose the following morning. Despite the waves that crashed over the deck all night, the curly-tail cage was still attached to the table. I wondered if anything or anyone else had been swept overboard. Did any animals get washed away? Apparently, the men were wondering the same thing, when they emerged onto the deck.

"Check the supplies and the haul," Bearded-Man said. The humans dispersed around the boat. Thin-Man came to the curly-tail cage, gave the side a whack with his hands, knocking the lizards about. "Hey, you guys still alive in there?" he asked.

I ran over hoping to be able to bite his finger through the cage, but couldn't reach him. The man laughed. He laughed at me!

"Hey, how 'bout you guys in here?" He bent down and lifted the lid on the box beside the table, the box where the thumping sound had come from the night before. I'd finally get the chance to see who was inside. "You didn't drown in that rainstorm, did you?"

"They okay?" asked Bald-Man as he came over.

"Yeah, they look okay. Angry, but okay." I ran to the other side of the cage and looked over the edge of the table.

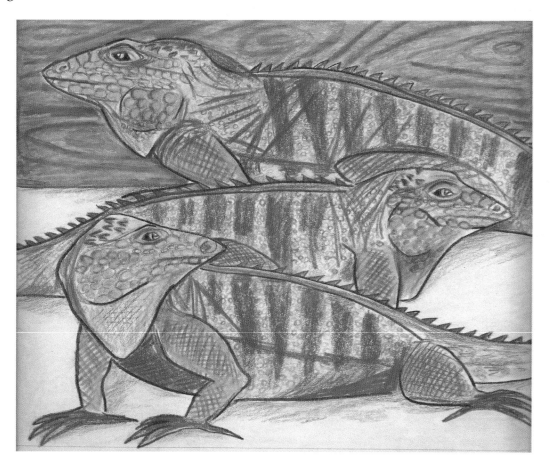

"What do you see?" Clive asked. Inside the box were several very large lizards. Their bodies were black but they had gorgeous red heads. One was definitely bigger than the rest. I wondered if that was the male.

"I don't know," I told Clive. "Hello, who are you? I'm Curtis Curly-tail of Warderick Wells."

The biggest of the lizards looked up at me.

"Hey, big guy, who are you?" I asked again.

"I'm not a guy. I'm a girl," stated the big lizard. I waited as she looked me over, cocking her head to one side and then the other.

"I'm Allison Iguana. I'm from Andros."

"Andros? Where's Andros, Curtis?" Clive asked. "Is it a city like Nassau or an island like Warderick Wells?"

"I don't know," I replied.

"Don't you curly-tails know anything about the Bahamas, the country you live in?" Allison said.

"Of course we do. But we have very short, but perfectly sized legs, so it takes us a while to get anywhere. Have you been to Warderick Wells?"

"No, why would an Andros Iguana, such as myself, deign to go to the Exumas?"

"To meet your neighbors?"

"Hey, check the hold," said Bearded-Man. Thin-Man opened the latch to the hold in the deck.

"All dry in here." He reached down and pulled up a plant. I'd never seen any plant like it. It had long thin leaves that were rounded at the ends.

Clive looked hopeful. "I wonder if they are edible! Maybe they brought those along to feed the iguanas. If iguanas like them, I bet I would, too."

"Iguanas wouldn't eat those," replied Allison. "Those are cycads. They are only good for humans and hermit crabs."

Bearded-Man peered into the hold. "Good, don't want to lose those plants. We're getting the most money for them."

"How come?" asked Thin-Man.

"They're some old kind of plant, a 'living fossil.' They were around with the dinosaurs," replied Long-Hair.

"Never seen a fossil that grows green."

Long-Hair came over to the hold.

"This, gentlemen, is the *Zamia lucayana*, also known as Bay Rush," he said.

"Lucayan. Say, weren't they the Indians who lived in the Bahamas first?" asked Bald-Man.

"You are correct. Many wondrous things are found in the Bahamas."

"I wish we could have stayed longer on Long Island. That was some great party we were having on the beach," said Thin-Man.

"Yeah, that island is long and thin like you, man," said Long-Hair.

"I was going to explore the big cave, too," Thin-Man added.

"Ah, business before pleasure, mate. Let's check out the rest of the boat, make sure nothing was damaged in the storm," said Bearded-Man. The lizards watched as the men walked around the deck.

"Do you think they're going to feed us, Curtis?" Clive asked.

"I don't know. I hope so." I replied, remembering all the times I had been hungry onboard humans' boats.

"Hey, I'm hungry. How about I catch us some fish for lunch?" asked Thin-Man.

"What are you going to use as bait?" asked Bald-Man.

"I noticed one of them curly-tails was scrawny. He ain't goin' to fetch much money. I thought I'd use him."

"Good idea. You'll get a big fish with him."

Thin-Man walked over to the cage holding us curly-tails. He opened the top and reached in.

I shouted to my friend, "Run, Clive, he wants to use you as fish bait."

The curly-tail lizards all crammed together in the corner farthest away from the approaching hand. They weren't trying to shield Clive but he squeezed himself between them and deep into the corner until he was on the very bottom of the pile of lizards.

The man pushed his hand in farther, scattering the lizards throughout the cage. I thought about biting the hand, when I realized there was a gap between the top of the cage and the man's arm. The perfect space for a perfectly sized curly-tail and his friend.

"Look up, Clive, we can escape out the top," I said. Clive looked up to see where I was pointing at the opening. With a surprising burst of speed, he jumped on the man's arm and ran up and out of the cage. Thin-Man lunged after him with his free hand, almost pulling the curly-tail cage off the table.

"Go, Clive, go!" I quickly followed my friend up and out, onto the wall and down to the boat's deck. I ran the in the opposite direction, as Thin-Man pushed the cage back onto the table. He pulled his arm out of the cage and closed the top.

He dashed around looking for Clive and me but we scurried from place to place. We ran to the bow and he followed. We ran down the deck on the other side of the boat and he still followed. He made one lunge for Clive and almost caught him.

"We need to hide. They'll catch us if we stay out in the open running," I said. The nice thing about being a perfectly sized curly-tail is that there are so many hiding places. I found a perfect space behind the box against the cabin wall, where Allison and her iguana friends were being held.

"Man, you let him get away," Bald-Man said to Thin-Man.

"Them lizards are fast! I'll grab another one," said Thin-Man, panting.

"No, leave them alone; we can catch them later," Bearded-Man said, leaning over the railing, looking into the water. "I see some nice conch below." Eagerly, Thin-Man and Bald-Man dove overboard and soon they were handing up conch after conch. Big conch, little conch, until the pile reminded me of a sand dune. Several of the conch extended their feet and were trying to escape back over the side. "Put them in the fish well." Thunk, thunk, the conchs fell one by one into the fish well.

"Hey, how about this for lunch?" Thin-Man held up an enormous lobster.

"Lobster for lunch, it is."

"Too bad, lobster season is over… Good thing we don't care!" said Bald-Man.

"Yeah, we'll just have to eat the evidence," Bearded-Man said. The men all laughed and prepared their lobster feast.

"Psst, Curtis. Where are you?" I heard Clive call.

"I'm over here behind the iguana box." Clive scurried down the wall to join me behind the box.

"What are we going to do now?" he asked.

"We're going to wait for the perfect moment to escape."

The boat continued on its journey. We curly-tails snacked on flies attracted by the lobster debris. An early evening shower rinsed the evidence of the lobster poaching off the deck into the sea.

All night long the boat continued north. Finally, the first rays of the morning sun sneaked into the crevice where Clive and I slept or, rather, had tried to sleep.

The men ate their breakfast on deck. Fortunately, it was grits and tuna fish, with the tuna fish coming out of a can. I was glad I didn't have to see one of my fellow animals captured and eaten. Between bites, they talked and laughed.

"Hey, man, did you see how I wrestled that big male iguana? I was like, swoop with the net, then I pinned him to the ground and whipped him into the bag. He must be at least twelve kilograms. We should be able to get top dollar. Maybe ten thousand Euros. That European guy buying this load is going to pop his eyes when he sees what we got for him. We got iguanas, we got curly-tails, we got conch for the feast, we got those plants he wanted. Man, we got 'im everything," boasted the Thin-Man.

"That weren't no male iguana. That's a female," Long-Hair said..

"You sure?"

"Yeah," said Bearded-Man. "But the breeder will be happy. He wanted females for his breeding business."

"Well, maybe we should go back and get him a big male, too. I'm the iguana wrestler," suggested the Thin-Man, showing the muscles in his arms.

"He's going to pay us so much, we can all retire and eat all the grouper and lobster we want whenever we want. The police haven't caught us and they won't. We won't care about it not being in season for anything," said Bald-Man.

As the morning turned to afternoon, the deck grew hotter and hotter. Even the shaded air in the crevice between the box and the boat's wall became uncomfortably hot.

I could hear a large body moving inside the box. I couldn't contain my curiosity. Maybe there was enough room for me to squeeze under the lid. I pushed my perfect body under the edge. In the dark box, I could see the shapes of the iguanas in the light shining through gaps in the lid.

"Psst, Allison," I said. "Clive and I escaped from our cage. We're going to help you escape, too."

"I don't think I need your help, little curly-tail," Allison responded. "The men surprised me before with their nets but I won't be surprised again."

"Curtis," Clive whispered, "I think that man is going to open the lid." Sure enough, daylight poured into the box. I scurried onto the side of the box to avoid being squished by the opening lid. I looked up in time to see the large female iguana leap onto the top edge of the box. Iguanas can jump!

"Hey, she's getting out!" yelled Long-Hair. "Close the lid!"

"No, you'll damage the iguana," Bald-Man shouted. "Just grab her."

"I'll catch her," Long-Hair said. He reached out with his hands to grab Allison around her neck. The iguana swung her tail up, flipped her head to the right, and bit down on the man's hand with all her might.

Blood gushed from Long-Hair's hand. He yanked his hand back out of the iguana's still closed mouth, shredding his skin and tissue on her razor sharp teeth. More blood gushed, making a mess all over the deck. Allison continued to roll, whacking him with her strong tail, removing even more skin.

"I'm going to chop her fool head off," said the Thin-Man, pulling a knife out of his pocket. "I know some great recipes for grilled iguana."

Bearded-Man used the distraction of the rising knife to grab the iguana. I leapt onto the man's beard, startling him. With a frightened shout, he jerked back, loosening his grip on the iguana. The iguana spun in a crocodile roll right out of his hands and landed on the deck. Her claws scrabbled on the deck but she moved her body forward until she found the edge of the rail fitting. With one last flip of her tail, she pushed herself forward over the side and into the water. I leapt off the beard, aiming for the deck, but I fell into the storage box instead. I hid underneath the iguanas' bodies. The iguanas all had their heads tilted upwards, mouths open with their impressive teeth showing. No human would reach in here to grab me.

I hoped Allison could swim well enough to reach a cay. I heard Thin-Man call for a net. "I could swim after her," he suggested.

"No way you'd catch her. Look at her go," Bearded-Man said. They watched as the iguana swam rapidly away, her powerful tail propelling her through the waves.

Clive climbed to the box's edge and dropped in next to me. "Are you okay?"

"Yes," I said, sitting on one of the remaining iguanas.

"You were magnificent."

"But we're still trapped," I replied. "But maybe not for much longer. If Allison can get off this boat, maybe we can, too. We'll just have to come up with another way to get to shore since we can't swim."

The men were so busy wrapping the injured hand in a towel that they forgot to close the lid on the box. The smaller iguanas looked hopefully at me. "Don't worry, friends. I'll think of something."

Eventually, Long-Hair stopped crying and the other men started blaming each other for the lost iguana.

"You know you have to hold an iguana at the neck and the hips."

"My hands couldn't reach around her neck," Long-Hair retorted.

"Then you should have left her to me," said Thin-Man.

"So why didn't you volunteer to grab her?"

"You didn't let me."

"Maybe she'll drown," said Bearded-Man.

"Doubt it, iguanas can swim. How do you think they got to all the islands?" said Long-Hair. "We still got the smaller iguanas and lots of other stuff. Maybe we can pick up another female iguana along the way. Maybe one not so big or so angry."

"But I caught that one, man, and you just let her jump over board," Thin-Man complained.

"You call getting my hand shredded, just letting her go?" snapped Long-Hair. "I'm lucky to still have my fingers."

"It's your own fault," said Thin-Man.

I was hoping the men would keep fighting until the rest of us kidnapped animals could figure out how to escape, too.

No matter how hard I thought, my perfect mind couldn't come up with a way to get the iguanas out of the box, the conch out of the fish well, and the other curly-tails out of the cage. The plants were on their own. I couldn't help them. I watched forlornly as the men sat around the deck.

"Hey, man, what's to eat? How 'bout some conch? We got plenty of conch," said Thin-Man. He reached into the fish well and pulled out a big conch with a large flaring lip which extended out from the curled part of the shell. The shell was a lovely cream color but the lip was a deep pink. The conch looked heavy and was almost half the length of the man's arm. It was the biggest shell I had ever seen. This must be a perfect conch. He reached in again, pulling out a smaller conch that barely had any lip at all, and put both of them on the table next to the curly-tail cage.

Coming a little ways out of my hiding place, I yelled to the conch, "Watch out! They're going to eat you. They tried to eat the iguana, but she escaped."

"I know," said the big conch. "People have been eating my kind since we first met."

The young conch kept his operculum tightly closed, doing his best to block out the realities of the world, I supposed.

"Which one should we eat? This one has lots of meat," said Thin-Man, pointing to the large conch.

"Yeah, but the little one is below minimum size. We'll attract unwanted attention if they catch us with him. Let's eat that one and save the big one for the customer," said Bald-Man. "This little

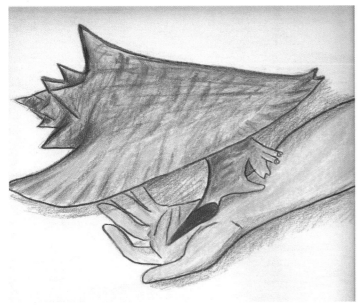

one will make a good chowder." "I can't let that happen," said the bigger conch. "I'm old with only a short time left any way. Help me save him, lizards."

"Of course, but how?" I asked.

"When I say 'now,' you help get him off the deck," said the old conch.

"But he's up on the table with you. How is he going to get down to the deck?" I asked.

"Watch."

Bearded-Man reached for the big conch to put him back in the fish well. The conch thrust out his foot, jabbed the man's hand with the edge of his hard, thin-edged operculum and pushed up his shell, as high as he could. The big conch's shell rammed the younger conch with enough force to knock him off the table.

The young conch landed with a thump on the deck. Bearded-Man cried out as the big conch continued to push the edge of his operculum into the man's palm, slicing deeper, causing blood to flow.

"Now, lizards, help the little one!" called the old conch, just before Bearded-Man hit his shell with a hammer. The shattering of the shell spurred us curly-tails into action. We reached the younger conch, just as he extended his foot.

"No, stay closed up, we're going to roll you overboard," I yelled.

The little conch clamped his operculum shut. Clive and I lined up along the shell and pushed. The conch rolled over easily until it hit the lip, little as it was, then stopped.

"We have to get it over the lip edge, Clive. I'll go underneath and lift." I jammed myself under the shell and pushed up.

"Roll him now, Clive." Clive pushed as hard as he could and the conch rolled over again. "One more time." This time the shell was close enough to the edge of the deck that his weight carried him over and into the ocean.

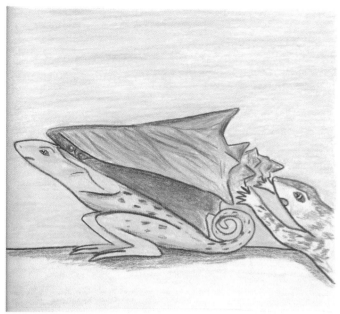

"Thaaank youuuu," came up with the bubbles, as the conch gently drifted to the bottom. Clive and I watched the sinking shell for almost a moment too long. A shadow passed over as one of the men grabbed for us. We ran for our lives to the bow of the boat.

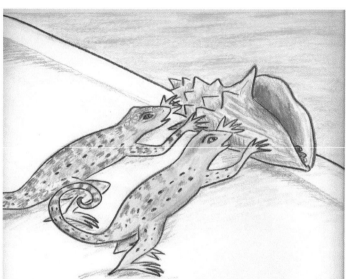

"We can't jump off. We're curly-tails, we'd be fish bait. We can't swim to shore," Clive cried.

"No, but we can run and we can hide again," I replied.

The men continued to chase us, reaching into crevices just after we'd run to another hiding place. Clive and I would run in opposite directions then suddenly change course back to each other. No matter where the men were, we were somewhere else. We could hear them swearing. Such inappropriate language, these humans used.

"What's going on, man? Why are all the animals getting away?" asked Thin-Man.

"Well, not all of them," replied Bearded-Man, wrapping a towel around the hand the conch had stabbed. "I'm going to enjoy eating this one." He cleaned the old conch's meat from his body. Even with his cut hand wrapped in a towel, he worked quickly, chopping the old conch's meat into small pieces. Fragments of the beautiful shell littered the table. Clive sneaked over to the pile and grabbed a piece with his mouth. He dragged a shard back to the cage. We watched sadly as the men cooked and ate the body of our friend. Clive pushed other pieces close to the cage for the other curly-tails to see.

"I'm so hungry," said Clive. "But I want to get off this boat even more than I want to eat. Can you think of some way for us to get off this boat?"

"I've always used shoes but I don't think that is going to work with these men. But I'll think of something," I said. I hope I'll think of something, I said only to myself.

The men ate their food quietly, occasionally speaking angrily to each other. The injured men winced when they used their hands. Harsh words were muttered.

"These troubles are a bad omen," said Long-Hair.

"Don't be stupid," replied Thin-Man. The men finished their meal and moved away from each other on the deck.

While the others went inside the cabin, Long-Hair checked the storage compartments making sure the remaining animals were still alive and still secure. Then he sat down on the box containing the iguanas and slept there the entire night. His hair fell against the curly-tail cage. Several of the lizards tried to pull it through the mesh to pull it out, but the man slept, occasionally moaning.

I kept a lookout at the front of the boat, but I didn't see any boats or docks or a way to make it to a cay. I'd prefer to go back to Warderick Wells, but right now I'd be happy to be on any land instead of this boat.

The next morning, the injured men were complaining a lot, saying they needed a doctor, whatever that was. The other men grumbled but one said he knew of a town with a doctor. The boat changed direction.

Town, I could work with a town, I thought. There had to be a way to get onshore in a town. Clive and I could live off flies attracted to garbage. We'd be okay.

We finally approached an island, but the men waited until dark to pull up to a dock. It was a long way up to the dock from the boat. I didn't see a way to climb up, not even a ladder, but I refused to be discouraged. Maybe one of the men would have a large pocket we could jump into but no, no open pockets. The two injured men were helped off the boat and they disappeared down the dock into the dark.

"Keep a look out for the night guard," said Bearded-Man. The men still onboard were nervous, pacing back and forth on the deck as the night wore on.

"Can we get off the boat now?" asked Clive.

"Have patience," I told him.

"I'm good at patience. I used to wait a long time for an insect to come by my bush back home," he said.

The sun lightened the horizon. What am I going to do? The men would come back and I didn't know how to get off this boat.

The dock was too far away to jump to even with my perfect legs. Extending my perfect tail completely wouldn't allow me to reach up to the dock. The ropes that tied the boat to the dock were too thin and drooped into the water. No good. "I won't let this boat leave with Clive and me still aboard," I said to no one in particular.

Then I saw them. A few fishing boats were coming toward us. If they came close enough, Clive and I could jump onboard and go with them to shore.

"Clive, get ready. We're going to try to jump on one of those boats. They might be boats that go fishing down near Warderick Wells."

"What poor creature are they after now?" asked Clive as he positioned himself on the bow of the boat.

"I don't know, maybe… Hey, look, there's a loggerhead turtle swimming in front of that boat."

"Oh no, they're going to catch the turtle. Another fellow reptile is going to die," Clive cried. He peered intently at the approaching people. "Are those weapons in their hands?"

"Let me look," I said as I climbed up over Clive. "No, those are cameras and binoculars, all the tourists carry them. Wait, that's not a fishing boat, it's a tourist boat."

"A tourist boat like the ones that come to Warderick Wells?" Clive asked.

"Yes! That settles it, Clive, we're going to try to jump onto the tourist boat."

The poachers became more active and Bald-Man untied the boat from the dock. He ran to the wheel and started the motor. The boat eased away from the dock, heading to channel and the open ocean, but the route out to sea was blocked! More boats were coming into the channel. Even though they were mostly small boats, enough of them were gathering to completely block the channel. Could it be that other humans were coming to our rescue?

"I'm going to ram them," said Bald-Man. He revved the engine. The boat started moving forward. The sound of a siren rapidly approaching made him hesitate. Suddenly, the boat surged into reverse and spun around. Clive and I held on to the edge of the bow to avoid being thrown off. More boats were coming to block off the other direction. Ordinary boats of ordinary people. Local Bahamians were coming to rescue their wildlife!

Bald-Man put the boat into neutral and grabbed the cage with the captive curly-tails. Clive and I ran down the deck toward them.

"Get back," the man yelled to the boats around us. He held the cage over the railing, out over the water. "Move out of the way or I'll drop the lizards in the water! It'll be your fault when they all die." The approaching boats slowed down. "Clear a channel! We're coming through."

"Curtis, what are we going to do? The bad men are going to escape and we won't be rescued," Clive said.

I replied "Not if we can help it. Follow me." I ran up the cabin wall and launched myself in a perfect arc to the man's face. Clive opted to run up his leg.

"Get off," he shouted as he thrashed around. The cage was getting dangerously close to the edge again. We had to get him to swing his arm back into the boat.

Thump! The boat heaved sideways, sending the man sprawling, and the cage slid safely to the middle of the deck.

"Is he down? Are the captives all safe?" came a voice from the water. I ran to the edge of the deck and looked. There she was, the loggerhead turtle with three others. They'd rammed the boat! They'd saved my fellow curly-tails!

"Yes, he is and they are!" I called. "You did it. You pack quite a punch!"

Seeing the man fall, the tourist and fishing boats, joined by several police boats, quickly circled the poachers' boat. It was over. I ran over to the cage with my cousin curly-tails. "Is everyone all right?"

"A little battered and bruised, but we're okay," came the reply. I was relieved.

More boats with sirens arrived. "Look, Clive. It's the...wait, this is going to take a moment, the Royal... Bahamas... Police... Force... Harbor... Patrol. They're approaching the boat!" I shouted so he could hear me over the noise.

"Prepare for boarding," said a voice from the patrol boat. "Your injured crew members were taken into custody at the medical clinic." The remaining poachers put up their hands and glumly watched the police climb on board to arrest them.

"I hope they like their cages," I said sarcastically. I really hoped they disliked them as much as we, their captives, had disliked our cages.

"Serves them right. Yay for the good humans," said Clive.

"You know the humans had help, right?" said the turtle, raising her head from the water.

"Yes, they did. Thank you. But how did you know we needed help?" I asked.

"It was the most amazing thing! I was taking a leisurely swim when an Andros iguana named Allison swam by. It's not every day I come across an iguana swimming out in the sea.

"She told me about how poachers had captured some of our fellow reptiles and were holding them captive onboard this boat, so I got some of the girls together and we lured the tourist and local boats into the harbor.

"Of course, the humans will take all the credit. But we don't mind."

The humans scurried around for a while. The poachers were taken away by the police. The conchs were transported in aerated water and returned to the sea. The plants were oohed and aahed over and carefully packed for transport back to their island. I couldn't understand such excitement over a bunch of plants. Since the iguanas were obviously from Andros, they were taken back to their home. That left only us curly-tails. The tourists took many photographs of the caged curly-tails. They must not realize how much better we look free on a patch of sand. Clive and I kept close to our caged cousins; we didn't want to be left behind. Clive, having an inferior den to mine, was willing to stay in this town with such wonderful people but I was eager to return home. The humans debated which island we were from. I would have told them if they had asked, but nobody did. The humans had just decided to put us in a display in Nassau when I heard a human voice yell, "Warderick Wells, they're from Warderick Wells."

"How do you know?" one of the other humans asked.

"The poacher who was bitten by the iguana confessed. If we get them to Warderick Wells, then they'll probably find their way to their own territories."

"We can find our way home, can't we?" I asked Clive.

"Yes, we can," Clive replied.

℃

After a few hours on another boat, our human rescuers placed the cage of curly-tails on the beach of Warderick Wells and opened the door. All the curly-tails eagerly jumped out. Clive was the last one out, waiting in the corner until everyone else had left. I ran to a nearby bush and waited for him.

As we climbed up sand dunes of home, Clive turned off to go towards the end of the island where his territory had been. I had met him there some time ago, trying to survive amid dead bushes.

"Where are you going?" I asked

"Home," Clive said, his tail drooping "such as it is."

"Why not set up a new den around here? I have a large territory and I know the tourists would enjoy more curly-tails to entertain them."

"You think it would be okay?" he asked, hopefully.

"Okay? It would be great. We can go on more adventures and share posing duty for the tourists. I confess, some days, I feel less than perfect." Of course, I always felt perfect but I thought Clive needed some encouragement.

"We can annoy the gull by running in opposite directions!" suggested Clive.

"So much to do for a couple of perfect curly-tails," I agreed.

"Okay, I'll try it for a few days to see if I like it," Clive replied.

Soon I was asleep, my perfect curled body snug in my perfectly sized den. I dreamt I heard my name being called. I uncovered my ear from under my curled tail and heard my name called again from outside the den. I had no desire to leave my comfortable bed and go outside. I was happy in my den and in my den I was going to stay.

"Curtis, please come out, I need your help," the voice called.

If I didn't know better, I'd swear that was Clive calling. But why would Clive be calling to me in the middle of the night? I opened one of my perfectly closed eyes and saw…sunlight. It was morning. I had slept through the sunrise. I uncurled completely, crawled to the edge of the den's opening and peered out. Sure enough, there was Clive standing outside my den opening, holding a piece of seashell. It was iridescent pink and white. It reminded me of something.

"What is that?" I asked.

"It's a piece of Old Conch," Clive replied.

"A piece of Old Conch from the boat? Why do you have a piece of him?"

"I wanted to keep a piece of him near me. I was going to keep it in my den so I would always remember his bravery."

"So why is it outside my den?"

"Because I had a better idea."

"A better idea?" I asked.

"Yes," said Clive matter-of-factly. "But I need your help to carry it."

"Carry it where?" I asked. I was getting very curious.

"To the top of Boo Boo Hill. You know, where the humans leave pieces of driftwood and stuff to appease the sea gods. They leave those offerings so they are guaranteed safe sailing."

"I'm not certain I understand."

"After all Old Conch did for us, I want to be sure he'll have smooth sailing into the afterlife."

So Clive and I dragged the piece of shell up the hill to the top where boards with ships' names and various other items were piled in a heap.

"Let's put it on top," I said. We carefully scampered over the pile until we reached the very top. I could see for miles across the blue ocean.

"This is the perfect place," Clive said. "The sea gods will be able to see it clearly." We gently placed the piece of shell on top of the other offerings, a fragment of our friend, the noble mollusk, Old Conch. The piece of shell seemed to glow in the sunshine.

"Safe travels until we meet again," Clive said into the wind.

Safe travels to you, too, reader. Poaching of animals and plants is a serious problem, not only in The Bahamas, but worldwide. We all need to work together to live sustainably on this wonderful planet. Thank you for coming along on this journey with me. Curtis Curly-tail.

Notes

The animals in this book are only a few of the animals and plants being poached in The Bahamas.

Curtis Curly-tail is a Curly-tailed Lizard (*Leiocephalus carinatus*).

Allison is an Andros Island Rock Iguana (*Cyclura cychlura cychlura*).

The Andros iguana is one of seven types of iguanas found in The Bahamas.
All are critically endangered.

Other victims of poaching include:

Queen Conch (*Strombus gigas*)

Spiny Lobster or Crawfish, (*Panulirus argus*)

Loggerhead Turtle (*Caretta caretta*)

Cycad (*Zamia lucayana*), endemic to The Bahamas

Glossary of Words

Andros: an island in The Bahamas, the largest of the inhabited islands. Home to the magnificent, colorful Andros Island Rock iguana, *Cyclura cychlura cychlura*.

Autotomy: a lizard's ability to drop part of its tail when grabbed by a predator. The tail continues to wiggle to distract the predator while the lizard escapes.

Boo Boo Hill: high point on Warderick Wells. Legend says it is haunted: Boo Boo refers to the voices heard on the wind on moonlit nights. Sailors leave an offering at the top of Boo Boo Hill to ask for good sailing and safe passage.

Deign: an action unworthy of a superior being

Exumas: a region of The Bahamas, consisting of 365 islands or cays. Site of the Exuma Cays Land and Sea Park.

Hermit Crab: a crustacean, such as the Caribbean Hermit Crab (*Coenobita clypeatus*) that uses an empty snail shell to protect its soft body.

Lizardnap: to steal or carry off a lizard

Lucayan People: first inhabitants of The Bahamas

Operculum: a hard structure that acts like a door on a snail's shell, like a conch. It is attached to the foot of the snail.

Thermoregulate: a reptile, like a lizard, does not produce his own body heat and his body temperature depends on the environment. He uses the environment to change his body temperature, such as basking in the sun to warm up and going into the shade or underground to cool off.

Warderick Wells: an island in the Exumas where the headquarters for the Exuma Cays Land and Sea Park is located. The home of Curtis and Clive.

Acknowledgments

Many thanks to my critique group members: Brad Peterson, Pamela Bickell, and Kate Steele for their guidance and creativity. Thank you to Dr. Charles Knapp for his scientific consultation. None of my books would be possible without my editor: thank you, Nora Miller. And thanks to Atlas Anderson for the cover art.

I am delighted to have artist and illustrator Jessica Minns, a Bahamian, join this Curtis Curly-tail adventure.

Other Curtis Curly-tail adventure books:

Available on Amazon and at major book sellers everywhere.

Curtis Curly-tail and the Ship of Sneakers
Curtis Curly-tail Hears a Hutia

Other books by Elaine A. Power:

Available on Amazon and at major book sellers everywhere.

Don't Call Me Turtle!

Made in the USA
Charleston, SC
17 October 2016